Steve Parish™

QUEENSLAND

CELEBRATING THE NATURE OF AUSTRALIA

Contents

▶▶

page 1: The Crimson Rosella is a colourful broad-tailed parrot that feeds on fruit and seeds. *pages 2 and 3:* Point Lookout, North Stradbroke Island. *left:* The exquisite Cooktown Orchid, proclaimed Queensland's floral emblem in 1959, occurs naturally in the northern part of the State.

Introduction

▶ ▶

Queensland, proclaimed an independent colony in 1859, is the second biggest State in the Commonwealth of Australia and covers nearly two million square kilometres. Through the last decades of the twentieth century and into the twenty-first its population grew fastest of all the States, passing four million in 2005.

Queensland's landscape is a varied palette of colour and natural beauty. The State's long coastline is bordered by blue-green seas, where stretches of reef nurture a treasury of marinelife and coral. Islands are heavily cloaked in dense rainforest that stretches right to the water's edge. On the mainland magnificent beaches give way to fertile coastal plains and ordered fields, rising to the cloud-veiled heights of the Great Dividing Range. Inland are towering temperate forests, wild rivers, rugged cliffs and seemingly endless parched deserts of red earth and rock.

Large areas of Queensland are considered ecologically important enough to have been inscribed on the World Heritage List: the Gondwana Rainforests of Australia, including Lamington National Park; Fraser Island; the Great Barrier Reef; the Wet Tropics, including the Daintree; and the Riversleigh Fossil Mammal Site are all protected areas.

Queensland wears her heritage proudly. Aboriginal tribes lived in Queensland's favourable climate for many thousands of years before European seafarers explored its coastline, and numerous rock art sites are testament to their long association with the land. In late 1824 British soldiers and convicts arrived at Redcliffe on the shores of Moreton Bay. And so began the intensive settlement and land-clearing that spread up the coast, across the ranges and over the plains. Pastoralists herded livestock and raised crops, and miners flocked to the goldfields.

Today Queensland is a favourite holiday destination for both Australian and overseas visitors. However, it is much more than that. It is a lifestyle — one that is relaxed and close to nature. Queensland is many worlds in one. It is a dynamic State, rich in creativity, natural beauty, history and adventure, just waiting to be explored, experienced and enjoyed.

left: Mount Maroon on the Scenic Rim, South-East Queensland.

Brisbane and Surrounds

Brisbane, the capital, is often called the River City as life centres on the Brisbane River's meandering course. John Oxley surveyed the river and Moreton Bay in 1823, suggesting that Redcliffe would be an ideal site for a penal settlement. In 1825 the convicts were moved from Redcliffe to the shores of the Brisbane River, where the fresh water supply was better, and work began on permanent buildings. In 1828 a vegetable garden was established on a loop of the river beside the fledgling town; the expanse of land came to be known as Gardens Point, and, in 1855, the City Botanic Gardens were opened there.

As ships were the only means of communication with Sydney and the rest of the world, the river was critical to the settlement. In 1842 the colony was opened to free settlers but traces of the convicts' labours remain in the Commissariat in William Street and the Old Windmill in Wickham Terrace, built as a treadmill to grind grain.

Brisbane gained importance as a port when surrounding areas were cleared, first through timber-getting and then for agriculture. But in reality Brisbane was two towns, one on the south bank and one on the north, until a temporary wooden bridge was opened in 1865. The first Victoria Bridge was finished in 1874 but was washed away in the huge flood of 1893. The bridge's existence, and then its absence, proved to the colony's populace just how much it depended on cross-river access. At least ten bridges for motor vehicles, trains and pedestrians now span the Brisbane River between the Gateway and Centenary Bridges.

Over the years Brisbane and the surrounding areas underwent cycles of boom and bust, following the economies of the rest of the world. But every boom time left the city larger and stronger, and more able to ride out times of hardship. Through it all the city kept its air of intimacy and friendliness. It was sometimes criticised for being "just a big country town" — the people of Brisbane would nod contentedly and agree.

This relaxed, subtropical haven and thriving business community has grown and matured into a beautiful, active, laid-back city of great charm and character. Around it lie the cities of Ipswich and Logan, and the communities of Pine Rivers, Deception Bay and the Redcliffe Peninsula. To the east the river empties into Moreton Bay, a bewitching mix of deep, open water, narrow channels, mangroves and forested sand islands.

left: The best way to travel along the Brisbane River's serpentine path through the city is to catch a CityCat.
pages 10 and 11: The Story Bridge, opened in 1940 to connect Kangaroo Point and Petrie Bight, sparkles with light against a sunset sky.

The River City

Joggers sweat, dog-walkers zigzag behind their charges, striders puff, families ramble and some just wander along beside the Brisbane River, the life-force of the city.

The parks and walks along the river draw thousands on weekends, during holidays and on long summer evenings.

Across the South Brisbane Reach from the city lies the cultural heart, comprising the State's library, museum, art gallery, performing arts complex, conservatorium and maritime museum. Beside these are the South Bank Parklands, created on the grounds where World Expo 1988 was held.

Pedestrians and cyclists stream between the two banks on the Goodwill Bridge and the footpaths beside the Victoria Bridge. On the northern bank, a bikeway and the floating RiverWalk run from the St Lucia campus of the University of Queensland to New Farm, downstream of the city. Along the way are the Regatta Hotel, City Botanic Gardens, Eagle Street Pier, the Old Customs House and New Farm Park, with cross-river ferry terminals, and stops for the CityCats along the way.

above, clockwise from top left: Paddlewheelers moored at Eagle Street Pier; the Goodwill Bridge is a cyclist and pedestrian bridge that connects Gardens Point with South Bank Parklands; CityFerries, though not as sleek and fast as CityCats, are a charming way to travel across Brisbane River; a cyclist at Riverside, with the Story Bridge in the background.
opposite: The lagoon and beach at South Bank Parklands were created for the 1988 World Expo.

top: Roma Street Parkland on the city's western rim, formerly the site of railway yards and the old Brisbane Markets, is the newest of the metropolitan parks.
above, left to right: The rotunda in New Farm Park; inside the Tropical Display Dome, Brisbane Botanic Gardens, Mount Coot-tha.

Gardens and Green Spaces

Walter Hill, the first curator of the City Botanic Gardens, trialled many plants from around the world to test whether they could be grown commercially in Queensland. He laid the foundation for this lush park, now past its 150th birthday. Work began in 1970 on a new, flood-free botanic gardens at the foot of Mount Coot-tha, and the gardens opened in 1976. They feature a series of gardens arranged in themes and geographical displays, including the 27-hectare Australian Plant Communities collection.

Bushwalkers and birdwatchers love Brisbane Forest Park, which begins at Mount Coot-tha, extending north-west; some of the walking trails pass through the rainforests of Mount Nebo and Mount Glorious.

left and above: The lush grounds of the City Botanic Gardens; the Rainforest Walk in Roma Street Parkland.

Historic Brisbane

Brisbane's architecture is a lively juxtaposition of historic buildings sitting gracefully beside modern office blocks and apartments. The blend of leafy suburbia, with its houses creating a timeline from the classic wooden colonial to the modern, and the city centre, with its subtle sprinkling of heritage buildings, helps to make Brisbane one of the world's most liveable cities.

Architectural examples from the nineteenth and early twentieth century are scattered through the CBD. On Ann Street, Australia's fallen soldiers are memorialised by the eternal flame of the Cenotaph, below which is the Shrine of Remembrance. At the corner of Alice and George Streets, with a pleasant view of the City Botanic Gardens, sits the French Renaissance-style Parliament House, which dates from 1868. Also on George Street are the Mansions, six terraced houses built in the 1890s of redbrick and sandstone. For some years Dr Lilian Cooper, Queensland's first female doctor, lived and practised there. The best view of Brisbane City Hall with its 92-metre clocktower, which was opened in 1930, is across King George Square.

A few buildings and civic works from the days of the penal colony remain. One of the most striking is the Old Windmill on Wickham Terrace, erected in 1828.

opposite, left to right: The Old Windmill; historic Naldham House is now home to the Brisbane Polo Club. *above, clockwise from top left:* Forgan Smith Building, University of Queensland, St Lucia; Brisbane City Hall seen across King George Square; the Mansions, George Street; the Shrine of Remembrance, Anzac Square.

top: South Bank Parklands is one of Brisbane's most popular relaxation centres, with promenades, shops and a giant saltwater lagoon edged by beach.
above: A drive up to the Mount Coot-tha Lookout for coffee, a meal or simply for a splendid view across the city to Moreton Bay is always popular.

Community Life

The citizens of Brisbane are part of the one great community but, within that, they belong to one or more villages, clubs and groups that swirl together, giving life in Brisbane texture, shape and colour. Some of the oldest suburbs — Paddington, West End, Kangaroo Point, New Farm and Fortitude Valley — are the most distinctive, bubbling with life and variety and flowing into the city's space. Different cultures and interest groups live side by side, their members following their own customs and beliefs but inviting their neighbours to share times of celebration and commemoration. Thus the Greek Paniyiri Festival brings scenes from the Aegean to Musgrave Park, Chinese New Year awakens the lion dancers in Fortitude Valley, and in Inala the Stylin' Up Festival celebrates Aboriginal culture and artistic achievements. Throughout the year special interest groups and clubs hold events like the Medieval Fair, and food, music and writing festivals bring the community together to socialise, learn and celebrate.

Sporting clubs, service organisations such as Rotary, religious groups, theatre and craft associations, charities, medical support groups and research fundraisers all contribute to community life. They are the threads that connect residents and visitors alike in this bustling city, turning it into a warm and caring place to live, work and play.

top, left to right: Market day in the Brunswick Street Mall, Fortitude Valley; the Greek community celebrates Greek heritage and culture during Paniyiri. *left:* Young children participate in a sports event.

Ipswich and the Brisbane Valley

Ipswich is 30 kilometres south-west of Brisbane at the junction of the Brisbane, Lockyer and Fassifern Valleys. Made strong by mining, it was Queensland's first provincial centre, becoming a municipality in 1860. This makes it possibly the State's most historically interesting city, since it has more than 6,000 Heritage-listed sites.

Ipswich was the collection and distribution point for Darling Downs and Brisbane Valley produce in days past. It is also the birthplace of Queensland Railways — the first line ran from Ipswich to Grandchester. Where could be a better site for the Workshops Rail Museum?

For many years it was thought that Ipswich might be the capital when Queensland became an independent colony, but the greater accessibility of the port at Brisbane saw it take the mantle. Nonetheless Ipswich Grammar (1863) is the oldest secondary school in Queensland. The region's history is covered in self-guided walks and museums, while drives through nearby towns and countryside show the beauty, produce and past of these rich valleys.

top: Once a contender for Queensland's capital, Ipswich contains many fine heritage buildings.
above: Cabanda Station is a stopping point for the Rosewood Railway Museum vintage rolling stock.

top: Fertile land to the west between Brisbane and the ranges supplies bountiful produce. Here pickers harvest spring onions outside Gatton.
above: The Foundation Building at the University of Queensland's Gatton campus is a beautiful example of early Queensland architecture.

North Stradbroke and Moreton Islands

North Stradbroke, or "Straddie", as it is called by its friends, is well known for holidays filled with surf, sun and sand. Humpback Whales pass close by the eastern surf beaches on their migrations to and from the Great Barrier Reef. In the quiet of the bay, to the west, turtles and Dugongs cruise in the clear, blue-green water. Migratory waders feed on the sandflats in summer; terns, gulls and pelicans live there all year; sea-eagles, Ospreys and exquisite Brahminy Kites wheel high overhead. Inland, the island's forests and freshwater lakes — Blue Lake, Tortoise Lagoon and Brown Lake — are habitat for many species of birds and animals. Oodgeroo Noonuccal, one of Australia's great poets, was born on North Stradbroke, a place she loved all her life.

Moreton Island, directly to the north, lacks paved roads and is almost entirely national park, which makes it a natural haven. Sandhills loom over forests, lakes, swamps and beaches; all these niches provide for prolific bird, animal and plant life. Sealife also thrives: Bottlenose Dolphins visit tourists at Tangalooma and frolic for a meal of fish, and on the western side lies a line of artificial reefs that shelter colourful fish, attracting scuba divers.

above, clockwise from top: Point Lookout on North Stradbroke Island is a good place to watch migrating Humpback Whales; standing atop the cliffs of North Gorge, Point Lookout, above the pounding sea; Brown Lake, North Stradbroke Island.

above, left to right: The old whaling station of Tangalooma, Moreton Island, is now a family resort where the local Bottlenose Dolphins delight visitors; Cape Moreton Lighthouse was built in 1857 and is still operational.

Toowoomba and the Golden West

The Golden West is a highly productive agricultural region. It stretches north-west from Toowoomba along the Warrego Highway and takes in the Eastern and Western Downs and Southern districts of the Condamine River basin. South again is the Granite Belt, famous for apples, pears, stonefruits and grapes.

Toowoomba, Australia's largest inland city and administrative centre for the rich and fertile Darling Downs, perches on the edge of the Great Dividing Range, 700 metres above sea level and 125 kilometres west of Brisbane. The city's elevation gives its air a crisp, invigorating tang. This was the heart of Cobb & Co. country until 1924 when the last coach ran from Surat to Yuleba. The Cobb & Co. Museum collection preserves the area's history and includes Australia's finest collection of horse-drawn vehicles. The Toowoomba Foundry, operational by 1876, sold the first of its famous Southern Cross windmills in 1903. Declared a municipality in 1860, Toowoomba has retained a good assortment of historic buildings, from the City Hall, built in 1900, to the Art Deco-style Empire Theatre. It has been dubbed the Garden City — a fitting name, especially in September when the city's 200-odd parks and gardens welcome spring during the Carnival of Flowers.

Queensland's oldest operating woolshed is at Jondaryan. It was built in 1859 on pastoral land in the heart of the Eastern Downs. Before the decline of truly large shearing sheds it held up to 52 blade-shearing stands and employed many workers; now it features demonstrations of shearing, blacksmithing and sheepdog trials.

Further to the north-west more of Australia's pioneering history is preserved at the Miles Historical Village. The main street holds a period blacksmith shop, bank and hotel, or visitors can marvel at the nineteenth-century school, dairy or police station. It also contains Aboriginal artefacts and relics from both world wars.

The Western Downs, where the Condamine River meets the Balonne, boasts of having some of the inland's best freshwater fishing. The nation's largest cattle saleyards are found here, at Roma. Heading south, the landscape changes again to pass through Goondiwindi, a major cotton and wheat-producing town, and to Stanthorpe in the cool Granite Belt, a wine and fruit-growing region near the Queensland–New South Wales border.

left: The fertile Darling Downs yields an abundance of crops and is Queensland's main grain-growing region.

top: The Lockyer Valley spreads in a magnificent panorama below the lookout at Picnic Point, Toowoomba.
above: The Royal Bull's Head Inn, Drayton, was the first pub on the Darling Downs and a post office for 50 years.
This building dates from 1858, but the original Bull's Head Inn was built in 1847–48.

top: Toowoomba's Queens Park is surely one of the loveliest sights imaginable when the spring blooms are out.
above, left and right: The Carnival of Flowers, first held in 1950, fills the last full week of September each year.

27

The National Parks of the Southern Downs

Cunninghams Gap, where the explorer Allan Cunningham crossed the Great Dividing Range north-east of Warwick in 1828, is situated in a pocket of wilderness known as Main Range National Park. Closer to the State's southern border are Sundown and Girraween National Parks, both places of remarkable beauty and havens for many species of wildlife. In Sundown National Park, layered rocks form steep gorges leading down to the Severn River. In Girraween, meaning "place of flowers" in the local Aboriginal dialect, the delicacy of spring wildflowers nestling among huge granite outcrops and balancing boulders delights the eye. The park provides protection for the rare Turquoise Parrot and the shy Superb Lyrebird with its excellent mimicry. This is also part of the restricted range of the much less familiar Albert's Lyrebird. Common Wombats are also found and all along the Scenic Rim Koalas can be spotted — occasionally even in roadside trees.

opposite: The southern end of the Queensland section of the Great Dividing Range is home to the Common Wombat.
above, clockwise from left: A Koala relaxes in a tree; Main Range National Park; open woodland of the Great Dividing Range.

above: The character of western Queensland in the early twentieth century is evoked by the sprawling verandahs and picket fences of these houses in Jandowae — and by the signature Bottle Tree.

Westward on the Warrego

The Warrego Highway leads west to the Outback. The important regional centres along it include Dalby, Chinchilla and Miles, all staging posts in the days of the Cobb & Co. coaches. As in most Queensland country towns, large hotels with deep, shaded verandahs have an allure that is hard to reject on a summer's day; their welcome must have been irresistible when travellers had spent hours jolting along pot-holed dirt roads in a swaying coach.

Dalby is in the heart of the Downs and its Pioneer Park Museum commemorates those who opened up the Golden West. Chinchilla, known as Australia's Melon Capital, produces almost a quarter of the nation's watermelons. The town is also noted for its Cypress Pine and attracts fossickers looking for petrified wood, known as "Chinchilla Red". Miles is particularly beautiful in September, being in the middle of a notable wildflower area, the blooms flourishing in early spring.

top: Dalby's Country Club Hotel.
above: The Jandowae Hotel, Jandowae.

The Southern Downs

Warwick, famous for its roses and its rodeo, is the main city in the Southern Downs. Its history dates back to the 1840s, and it is arguably the site of Australia's first rodeo, a spectacle that soon grew popular throughout Australia's grazing areas.

In Warwick's town centre the impressive Town Hall, built in 1888, and Post Office, built in 1891, are made from local sandstone. The city and surrounding district are scattered with splendid sandstone homesteads that date from the mid-nineteenth century.

In nearby Yangan the architecture is more practical than grand, incorporating shady verandahs ideally suited to Queensland's harsh summer.

South, past Warwick, lies Stanthorpe and the Granite Belt. High on the western scarp of the Great Dividing Range, frosts, chilling winter winds and occasional snow make this Queensland's coolest climate. The region is known largely for its fruit and wine production. The local vineyards are growing in number and prestige every year: more and more award-winning vintages can be traced back to the Granite Belt.

The area is flanked by national parks to the south that protect rare habitat and wildlife, as well as delighting park visitors with the scenery's majesty.

opposite: At Maryvale, near Warwick, an old farmhouse sags wearily on its foundations.
above, clockwise from top left: The Warwick Post Office; Warwick's sandstone Town Hall; the Yangan Masonic Lodge; the School of Arts building, Yangan.

The Western Downs

Roma is at the western edge of the Golden West and the eastern edge of the mulga and Mitchell Grass plains. Every year Roma hosts "Easter in the Country", a festival that attracts visitors from near and far and offers great country-style entertainment.

The people of Roma are known for their esteem for a good bushman. This attitude was displayed most strongly in 1872 when Harry Redford, the model for Captain Starlight in the Australian novel *Robbery Under Arms*, was tried in Roma for cattle duffing after his epic drive of a thousand stolen head from Bowen Downs, near Longreach, down through the Channel Country to South Australia. Despite strong evidence to the contrary, the jury, in awe of his feat, found him not guilty. (Legend has it that they added "but he should give the cattle back".) On a more sombre note, Heroes Avenue commemorates Roma's sacrifice during World War I — over 100 Bottle Trees line the avenue, each standing for a local soldier who did not come home from the war.

South-east of Roma, Goondiwindi — a name of Aboriginal origin meaning "resting place of the birds" — was home to Gunsynd, the punters' beloved "Goondiwindi Grey" racehorse. The main local produce is wheat, cotton, beef and wool and large olive plantations have recently been found to thrive in the dry climate of the region as well.

top: The majestic School of Arts Hotel, McDowall Street, Roma.
above: One of Roma's many Heritage-listed houses.

top: The old Customs House, Goondiwindi, which now houses the Goondiwindi Museum.
above: The Macintyre River flows through Goondiwindi and forms part of the Queensland–New South Wales border.

The Gold Coast and Hinterland

▶ ▶

The Gold Coast is named for the chain of sparkling sand beaches that stretches north from the Tweed River to the Spit at Southport. With an average daily temperature of 25° Celsius and close to 300 days of sunshine each year, Gold Coast City is home to almost half a million Queenslanders who love the climate, the lifestyle and the Pacific rollers foaming towards the magic beaches. When you add the theme parks, fishing, sporting fields, water sports, day trips and restaurants, it is not surprising that the Gold Coast is one of Australia's most popular holiday destinations.

Every Gold Coast beach has star quality, but first among equals is Surfers Paradise, which has been a family holiday resort since a wooden bridge was built across the Nerang River in 1925. Today, "Surfers" attracts droves of young people seeking holiday fun, families, committed shoppers and both domestic and international tourists.

The Broadwater's sheltered channels are excellent for boating and water sports, while its southern end is protected by the long stretch of sand known as the Spit. The Gold Coast Seaway, which separates the Spit from South Stradbroke Island, is the southern entry point to Moreton Bay. The upmarket shops, cafés and restaurants of Marina Mirage are found on the Spit, as are several luxury hotels and Seaworld, a popular marine theme park.

When the sun goes down, the Gold Coast lights up. The pace quickens as brilliant lights probe the night: Jupiter's Casino at Broadbeach shimmers like a dreamland; dancers move to music's beat in the Coast's many clubs and bars; and diners relax at the street cafés.

The Gold Coast Hinterland, the "green behind the gold", is clad with thick, rich volcanic soil and lush rainforest. Some of Australia's most diverse fauna and flora is found in this area, part of the World-Heritage-listed Gondwana Rainforests of Australia, as well as wet eucalypt forest, impressive rock formations and waterfalls that plunge into clear rocky pools.

Walking tracks criss-cross Lamington National Park, Australia's largest reserve of subtropical rainforest. Springbrook National Park, high on the Scenic Rim, is renowned for its clear mountain streams and ancient Antarctic Beech trees.

left: The Gold Coast is studded with high-rise buildings, but the imposing Q1 towers over them all.
pages 38 and 39: The view south-west over the Gold Coast from the Spit and Broadwater. The mountains of the hinterland are in the distance.

above, left to right: A walk on the beach is one of life's simple pleasures; the Broadwater is ideal for most types of water sport.
opposite: The mouth of the Tweed River marks the southern end of the Gold Coast. Here lie the twin towns of Coolangatta and Tweed Heads, on the Queensland–New South Wales border.

The Hinterland

Swathes of the hinterland, like the beautiful Numinbah Valley, are taken up by farming and similar pursuits, such as wholesale plant production for nurseries. Mountain villages like Tamborine have become popular with artists, craftspeople and boutique primary producers and vintners. Locals, near-locals and tourists take enjoyment in trawling through the galleries and shops in search of the perfect gift or souvenir. But the scenery and wildlife hold the key to the beauty and power of the hinterland.

above, left to right: A curtain of water plunges into the cavern beneath Natural Bridge; the colourful male Regent Bowerbird.
opposite: A young Red-necked Pademelon, just days after leaving its mother's pouch.

this page and opposite: Lamington National Park is one of the brightest treasures in South-East Queensland and part of the Gondwana Rainforests of Australia World Heritage Area. Each year thousands of visitors enjoy the 160 kilometres of walking tracks, admiring the outstanding valley and mountain views. Here are found Elkhorn, Staghorn and Crows Nest ferns and cascading waterfalls such as Elabana Falls, Morans Falls (this page, left and right) and Chalahn Falls (opposite).

The Sunshine Coast and Hinterland

▶ ▶

North of Brisbane, stretching from Bribie Island in the south to Noosa and Cooloola in the north, lies the Sunshine Coast. This coast combines with its hinterland to make one of the loveliest and most accessible regions in Queensland. The pleasure of holidaying or doing business on the Sunshine Coast is reflected by the annual visitor numbers: it attracts close on three million domestic and international visitors per year. Most come on holiday, but an increasing number of visitors come to attend conventions and conferences, as well as national sporting events, particularly golf tournaments and triathlons.

Settlement of coastal towns such as Noosa and Maroochydore followed the timber-getters who pushed into forest along the rivers in search of the massive Red Cedars that once abounded. Other commercially important trees were beech and pine — Hoop, Bunya and Kauri. River ports grew to ship the timber and off-load miners heading for the Gympie goldfields with their packs and supplies. Soon after, merchants and farmers followed these hopeful fortune hunters.

The plains between the coast and the mountains and the cleared country at the top of the ranges provide some of the richest agricultural land to be found in this ancient island. The volcanic soils owe their richness to the Glass House Mountains, the weathered remains from geothermal turmoil long ago. Tropical fruits, such as pineapples, bananas and passionfruit, as well as many exotic and less common fruits are grown here. The region also supports tomatoes, cucumbers and hydroponic lettuces and greens, dairy products, macadamia nuts and, in days past, sugar cane. Here also is Australia Zoo, the former headquarters of one of Australia's more famous sons, the late Steve Irwin, the Crocodile Hunter.

A wide range of habitats is encompassed by the coast and the D'Aguilar, Conondale and Blackall Ranges: rainforest, wet eucalypt forest, woodland, pine forests, rivers, swamps and lagoons, mangroves, wallum, heath and dune communities. Swathes of land are protected in national and environmental parks within and around the fast-growing urban landscape. Fringing this complex web of life to the east is a series of unsurpassed beaches on whose silver-gold sands break the long, rolling waves of the Pacific Ocean.

left: Looking from Bribie Island across Pumicestone Passage to the
Glass House Mountains silhouetted against the evening sky.

The Hinterland

Woodford, Maleny, Palmwoods, Montville and Mapleton have drawn artists, craft workers, writers and musicians who are inspired by the area's natural beauty and supported by the guild-like life of creative communities. Their artwork can be seen in galleries and souvenir shops in the towns, or in nearby Eumundi at the twice-weekly markets which are an arts and crafts extravaganza with an eco-friendly theme. Bed-and-breakfast cottages, ideal for romantic interludes or soul-restoring getaways, nestle in the forest or perch high on the rim of the ranges.

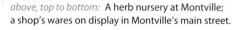

above, top to bottom: A herb nursery at Montville; a shop's wares on display in Montville's main street.

above: The 13 volcanic plugs of the Glass House Mountains rise up to 300 metres above the green hinterland. The British explorer James Cook named them as they reminded him of the glass-making furnaces in his native Yorkshire.

Caloundra to Coolum

Caloundra is a seaside resort popular with families as it has both sheltered bays and surfing beaches. Its historic lighthouse, owned by the National Trust, was built in 1898 and is the town's oldest structure.

Mooloolaba, a short drive away, is home to Underwater World and is the finishing port for the Auckland–Mooloolaba and Sydney–Mooloolaba yacht races. Maroochydore, just north of Mooloolaba, overlooks the estuary of the Maroochy River and, although one of the Sunshine Coast's largest shopping and commercial precincts, retains a relaxed, seaside town appeal. Further north Coolum is close to some world-class golf courses, and the rocky headlands and Mount Coolum provide spectacular views.

opposite: Point Cartwright, foreground, the Mooloolah River and Mooloolaba Beach.
above, clockwise from top left: Caloundra; Maroochydore; Coolum.

Noosa

Noosa is a cosmopolitan, stylish resort town of fine places to eat, shop, fish, surf, dive, walk and swim. Nearby Noosa National Park has unusual rock formations and walking tracks through the rainforest and around Noosa Headland. There are also tracks and paths along the winding Noosa River, which is dotted with islands and wetlands. The harmonious combination of Noosa's built and natural environments is testament to the determination of a small group of locals, such as author Nancy Cato who championed the protection of Noosa through the development-mad 1970s.

above, top to bottom: Aerial view of Main Beach, Noosa; Hastings Street, Noosa.
right: Sunlovers enjoy Main Beach and Laguna Bay.

pages 54 and 55: Cooloola Beach, at the northern end of the Sunshine Coast and part of the Great Sandy National Park, has become a four-wheel-drive motorway where road rules apply. Beach fishing is a regular activity here.

The Fraser Coast and Hinterland

The coast of the Wide Bay–Burnett district, extending north from the peaceful town of Tin Can Bay to the coastal city of Hervey Bay, is also known as the Fraser Coast, named after Captain James Fraser and his wife Eliza, who landed on Fraser Island after the shipwreck of the *Stirling Castle* in 1836. The landscapes are diverse. Protected from the open sea by Fraser Island, this stretch includes one of Queensland's oldest cities, Maryborough, on the Mary River.

Known as the Heritage City, Maryborough was established as a wool port in 1847 and later became an immigration port for free settlers. Maryborough's history is seen in the buildings of the Wharf Street precinct, which contains many Victorian and early colonial government buildings and houses. Just 34 kilometres away is Hervey Bay, famous as a place to view the annual migration of Humpback Whales along the east coast of Australia.

World-Heritage-listed Fraser Island, the largest sand island in the world, lies just off the coast. It is over a million years old and one of the few places where significant areas of rainforest grow on pure sand. The Butchulla people, whose association with the island goes back more than 5,000 years, called their home *K'gari,* meaning "paradise". Freshwater creeks run through lush green rainforest past glistening perched, barrage and window lakes, ranging from the palest blue-green to golden brown. Lake McKenzie, which covers more than 150 hectares, has spectacular aquamarine waters over a bed of soft white sand.

At least 354 bird species have been recorded on Fraser Island, including the endangered Ground Parrot, which is found in the wallum heath. The island and the Great Sandy Strait are important resting places for migratory waders on their long flights between southern Australia and their Siberian breeding grounds. The Dingos here are believed to have one of the purest bloodlines in Australia, and so are probably the closest living links with their predecessor, the Indian Wolf. Frogs, snakes, lizards, bats, possums, gliders, echidnas and Swamp Wallabies also live here. The seas are a haven for turtles, Dugongs and dolphins.

Inland centres on the Fraser Coast include Kingaroy, famous for its peanuts, and Gympie, a former gold-rush town. Bunya Mountains National Park is home to the most extensive Bunya Pine forests in the world.

left: Bigeye Trevally form dense schools. The Fraser Coast is known as one of Australia's finest fishing regions.

above, left to right: Fraser Island is 123 kilometres long, 30 kilometres across at its widest point, and spreads over more than 184,000 hectares; Wanggoolba Creek winds through the island's rainforest.

Hervey Bay and Fraser Island

Transformed over the years from a small coastal settlement to a bustling resort town, Hervey Bay has safe swimming and is ideal for fishing. Hundreds of migrating Humpback Whales seek out these calm waters on their yearly migrations. Delighted passengers on whale-watching tours can see them frolic and rest here as they journey between their Antarctic feeding grounds and their breeding grounds in the Great Barrier Reef region.

Fraser Island, rich in marine and terrestrial life, is the final, and largest, of the string of great sand islands built up on the Queensland coast by the Eastern Australian Sand River. This is a huge northerly flow of sand carried up the coast from the Tasman Sea by the Eastern Australian Current. North of Fraser the tidal flow from Hervey Bay banks the sand up to form Breaksea Spit, which extends 30 kilometres from the tip of Fraser Island to the edge of the continental shelf. Here the sand river spills over the shelf and is tipped 4,000 metres to the seabed.

above, top to bottom: Breaching Humpback Whales off Fraser Island; paperbarks surround one of Fraser's many lakes; a lone Dingo prowls the tideline.

Kingaroy to Gympie

Kingaroy is the peanut capital of Australia but is now forging a name for itself in viticulture; it is home to several quality wineries producing a range from chardonnay to shiraz. Kingaroy's Mount Wooroolin Nature Refuge is a must for birdwatchers, and waterbirds can also be spotted on nearby Gordonbrook Dam. To the north-east, Gympie's Gold Mining and Historical Museum commemorates the area's beginnings in the gold rush.

top: The Carrollee Hotel in Kingaroy is a grand example of the region's historical buildings that feature fine brickwork and stone detailing. *above:* Inside the Gympie Gold Mining and Historical Museum.

Maryborough

Maryborough is a historic city and contains many attractive examples of Victorian architecture. On Lennox Street, Brennan & Geraghty's Store, which first opened in 1871, is but one of Maryborough's fine commercial buildings; it is now preserved as a museum. The Railway Museum, appropriately housed in the old railway station, is also of particular interest. When the 1867 gold rush brought droves of fossickers and miners to Gympie, Walkers Foundry was built, establishing the city as an engineering base. Today timber, sugar and engineering remain Maryborough's largest industries.

top and above: Maryborough's streets are filled with well-preserved colonial buildings that hark back to the city's early days as a busy port.

The Bunya Mountains

Bunya Mountains National Park, south of Kingaroy, is home to the most extensive Bunya Pine rainforests in the world. More than 120 species of birds, mammals, frogs and reptiles live among the park's Bunya Pines, Red Cedars, figs, Bottle Trees and vine thickets. It is also a place of Aboriginal importance, where corroborees were held.

above, left to right: Red-necked Wallaby with joey; Bunya Pines in the national park named for them.
opposite: The Crimson Rosella is often found tame around campgrounds.

The Coral Coast and Central Queensland

▶ ▶

The Coral Coast stretches north from Bundaberg, through Gladstone, along the Capricorn Coast to Rockhampton. Bundaberg, just north of Hervey Bay, lies about 20 kilometres inland on the Burnett River, while the port is at the river's mouth. First settled as a farming and timber-getting outpost, the area has grown to be one of Queensland's great sugar-producing centres. Just north is Mon Repos Conservation Park, the most important mainland nest-site for sea turtles. Further north, Agnes Waters and Seventeen Seventy lie on the coast between Deepwater and Eurimbula National Parks. Seventeen Seventy was the first place on the Queensland coast where British explorer James Cook made landfall. The town's name commemorates the year of this event. From here the coast turns sharply north-west. Gladstone, the port for the central Queensland coalfields, is built around a natural deepwater harbour. Home to the largest alumina plant in the world and Australia's largest aluminium smelter, Gladstone is also a jump-off point for the southern reef. Further north-west is Rockhampton, Australia's beef capital, a subtropical city on the Tropic of Capricorn.

Offshore and 85 kilometres north-east of Bundaberg lies Lady Elliot Island, part of the Capricorn–Bunker island group and the most southerly island in the Great Barrier Reef Marine Park. For those travelling north it offers the first chance to see parts of this magical World-Heritage-listed coral reef system. North of Lady Elliot are Lady Musgrave Island and Heron Island. The latter is rated as being one of the best diving locations on earth. Since the early 1950s it has housed an internationally acclaimed research station run by the University of Queensland.

Central Queensland is geographically and scenically fascinating, with national parks that are invaluable in protecting Aboriginal and natural heritage. Carnarvon National Park holds pockets of remnant inland rainforest and significant galleries of Aboriginal rock art. Mount Etna Caves National Park is part of a limestone cave system that is the breeding site for 80 per cent of Australia's Little Bent-wing Bats and for the endangered Ghost Bat. These parks, along with Expedition National Park and the coastal parks, care for wide-ranging habitat types and wildlife communities.

left: Some of Australia's best shallow-water coral-reef diving is in the Capricorn–Bunker group of the Great Barrier Reef.

Bundaberg

The city of Bundaberg, founded in 1870, sits astride the Burnett River. Well known for sugar-cane production, it is the home of famous Bundaberg Rum. Local engineering works cater to the sugar and maritime industries. Poincianas, figs and bauhinias, which flower in spring and summer, bring colour to the city's wide streets. The many parks and gardens are also peaceful spots for reflection.

left: Bundaberg, on the Burnett River.
above: A Rainbow Lorikeet feeding in coastal she-oak.

above, left and right: Snorkelling and exploring the beach: just two of the ways to enjoy Heron Island,
a sanctuary for at least 30 species of seabirds, 900 species of fish, many corals and nesting turtles.

above, left to right: The waters of the Capricorn–Bunker group teems with sealife; Lady Musgrave Island shines like a jewel in the brilliantly blue waters of the southern Great Barrier Reef; a diver swims above schools of shimmering fish.
opposite: The reef's inhabitants share little but an astonishing diversity of colour, form, pattern and texture.
pages 72 and 73: A Bottle Tree, a characteristic silhouette of the Central Queensland inland, stands against the sunset.

Rockhampton

Established in 1853 on the Fitzroy River, Rockhampton is a graceful town with more than twenty attractive colonial buildings adorning the city centre. The city is surrounded by prime beef-grazing land and handles the largest throughput of export beef cattle in Australia. It is also the biggest stud-selling venue in the Southern Hemisphere. Six statues of bulls, representing the main breeds found in the area, are scattered through the streets. Nearby Mount Morgan was famed for its gold, silver and copper mines.

Mount Etna Caves National Park is to Rockhampton's north, on the Beserker Range. To the north-east, north of Yeppoon, the picturesque coastline of Byfield National Park overlooks Corio Bay. Here, Little Terns nest at Sandy Point and vulnerable Beach Stone-curlews have been sighted.

top: National Trust-listed buildings line Quay Street, Rockhampton.
above, left to right: The Criterion Hotel; Rockhampton's sandstone Post Office; Customs House, now Rockhampton's Visitor Centre.

The Gemfields

The Southern Hemisphere's largest sapphire deposits are found about 270 kilometres west of Rockhampton in the gemfields around Anakie, Sapphire and Rubyvale.

The first sapphire was found at Withersfield in 1870 but mining did not start in earnest until years later. Blue translucent corundum was considered "true" sapphire and other colours were called "fancy stone".

Nowadays the fields operate equally as commercial mines and as a tourist destination. Visitors to the region can fossick for sapphires of all colours and for semi-precious stones such as amethyst, ruby, topaz and zircon.

Contrary to images conjured by its name, the nearby town of Emerald was named for the rich colour of the landscape after rain rather than for precious stones.

this page: Images from Sapphire and Rubyvale, two of the State's most celebrated sapphire fossicking areas.

above: An aerial view of Byfield National Park and Corio Bay.

Capricorn Coast

Named for its proximity to the Tropic of Capricorn, the Capricorn Coast includes the southern islands of the Great Barrier Reef. Great Keppel Island, 1,454 hectares, is the largest in the Keppel group, and is just 15 kilometres east of Rosslyn Bay. It is famed for its 17 pure-white sand beaches.

The first European settlers came to Yeppoon in the 1860s. For more than a hundred years, the area was sustained by fruit growing, timber and cattle; now the town provides a relaxed lifestyle within easy commuting distance of Rockhampton, the Capricorn Coast's main city. Yeppoon is an unspoilt holiday destination offering largely undeveloped beaches and views of Great Keppel and North Keppel Islands. Nearby is Coo-ee Beach, the location of an annual coo-eeing competition. North of Yeppoon is Byfield National Park and Shoalwater Bay Military Training Area.

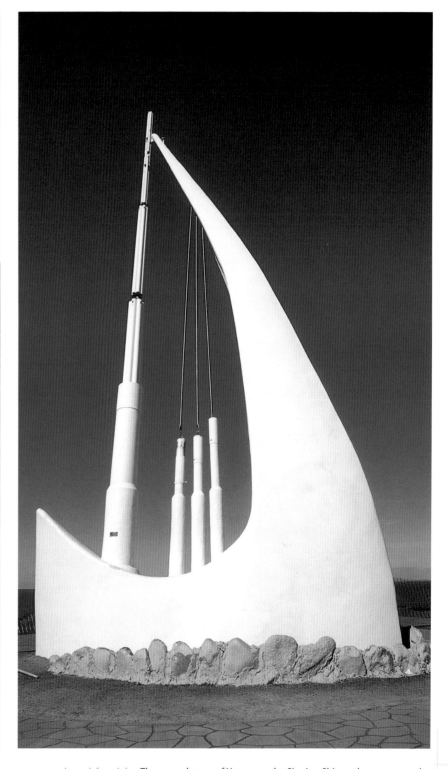

above, left to right: The coastal town of Yeppoon; the Singing Ship sculpture graces the headland above Keppel Bay and fills the air with music when the sea breezes blow.

above, left to right: Experienced bushwalkers will enjoy the Mount Moffat section of Carnarvon National Park, which has rugged and isolated walking trails as well as some easier tracks; sheer cliffs tower above Cabbage Tree Palms in Carnarvon Gorge. *opposite:* Cathedral Cave, Balloon Cave and the Art Gallery in Carnarvon National Park have some of the finest Aboriginal rock art in Australia.

Carnarvon Gorge

Carnarvon Gorge is the most accessible section of Carnarvon National Park, which covers 298,000 hectares. This chasm twists and turns for 30 kilometres between ancient sandstone cliffs, some 200 metres high. Cabbage Tree Palms, she-oaks and eucalypts grow beside Carnarvon Creek. Other flora of Carnarvon National Park include cycads and giant King Ferns dating back 300 million years. Carnarvon is a significant site in Aboriginal mythology. An extensive collection of fragile rock art, including stencils, engravings and freehand paintings, decorate the sandstone cliffs and caves. Very little is known of the people who lived here and consequently this collection of rock art, the largest in Queensland, is a precious historical and cultural link to the past.

Mackay and the Whitsunday Region

▶ ▶

From Bundaberg north the story of the coast also becomes the story of the Great Barrier Reef. Mackay is close to the quiet mystique of the softer-coloured inner reefs and the magic of the outer reefs. Yet it is also a city surrounded by a sea of sugar cane. It was first settled in the 1860s for cattle grazing and fattening, but now produces nearly a third of Australia's sugar. National parks to its north and west, such as Cape Hillsborough, are repositories for the region's original flora and fauna, notably lowland rainforest and vine forest. In Eungella National Park the wet tropical rainforest of the north meets the mountains. The Aboriginal people called this misty landscape the "Land in the Cloud".

Close by are the Whitsunday Islands, famous for being one of the greatest sailing and cruising grounds in the world. The Whitsundays are continental islands, the peaks of once-prominent mountains that were submerged when sea levels rose at the end of the last Ice Age. Dark green forests plunge down these steep-sided islands to stop abruptly at the snow-white beaches that fringe the land. The water shades from deepest peacock blue through turquoise to palest aqua where sandbars lie close to the surface. Even in the highest winds there are plenty of spots among the 74 islands that offer safe anchorage.

Bowen, famous for mangos, is on the coast at the northern end of the Whitsunday Group, just 40 minutes drive from Airlie Beach. North-west of Bowen the coal terminal at Abbot Point loads coal from the Collinsville mines in the Bowen Basin field.

South-west of Mackay sits the former gold-mining town of Clermont, one of tropical Queensland's oldest settlements. Jeremiah Rolfe, the first white settler, was in the district by 1856. Gold was found beside nearby Hoods Lagoon in 1861 and copper was discovered in 1862. However, the supplies were shortlived and the town's population soon declined from its mid-1860s peak of 3,500. Nonetheless the output of gold and copper, coal at Blair Athol as well as beef and sheep meant that the town would survive, even though it was forced to move to higher ground after devastating floods in 1916.

left: Mountainous Brampton Island is in the Cumberland Group of the Whitsundays, part of the Great Barrier Reef World Heritage Area.

above: Peak Range National Park, east of Clermont, is dotted with volcanic plugs.

Mackay

Mackay's picturesque marina is a pleasant place to watch the world go by or to enjoy first-rate alfresco seafood. The scenery is grand and the town has a palm-fringed main street, some beautiful historic buildings and a laid-back feel, yet it has all the trappings of a major regional centre. Mackay was named after the father of John Mackay, leader of the first colonial expedition to the Pioneer Valley in 1860.

above, clockwise from top left: Mackay is a blend of modern-day architecture and heritage buildings; Mackay's deepwater harbour enables sugar to be shipped around Australia; cane farms take advantage of the rich soil; Mackay, astride the Pioneer River.

Two Special National Parks

The scenery of Cape Hillsborough National Park is spectacular: magnificent Hoop Pines, eucalypt forest, wetlands, rainforest and beaches strewn with rhyolitic boulders. This diverse landscape is home to a variety of wildlife, including Eastern Grey Kangaroos and Agile Wallabies, which are often seen on the beaches at dawn and sunset. Equally lovely is Eungella National Park, where subtropical and tropical rainforests blend in a unique environment. Visitors may spot the rare and elusive Platypus, found in Broken River.

opposite: The emerald beauty of Eungella National Park, gazetted in 1941. In Eungella on the Clarke Range, the rainforest species from the Wet Tropics meet subtropical species from the Queensland–New South Wales Border Ranges area.
above, clockwise from top left: Cape Hillsborough National Park; Finch Hatton Gorge, Eungella National Park; a Platypus swims in Broken River, Eungella National Park; an Eastern Grey Kangaroo at Cape Hillsborough National Park.

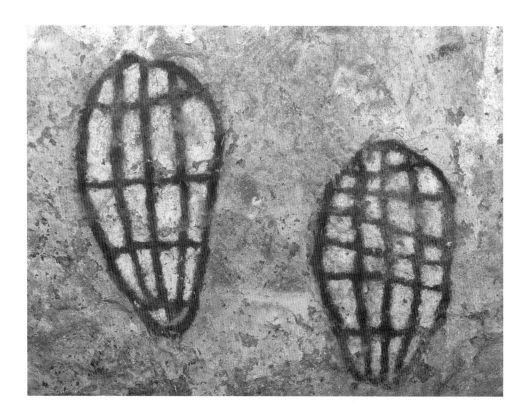

above, left to right: Coral-fringed Nara Inlet, Hook Island, provides perfect overnight anchorage and a secluded island experience; Aboriginal rock art on Hook island.

above, clockwise from top left: Looking over Hayman Island's luxury resort to Hook Island; Hamilton Island is the most commercially developed of the Whitsunday Islands; Airlie Beach, the area's lively tourism and administrative centre, is the gateway to the Whitsundays; from Shute Harbour cruise boats take visitors to explore the Whitsunday Islands or the beauty of the outer reefs.

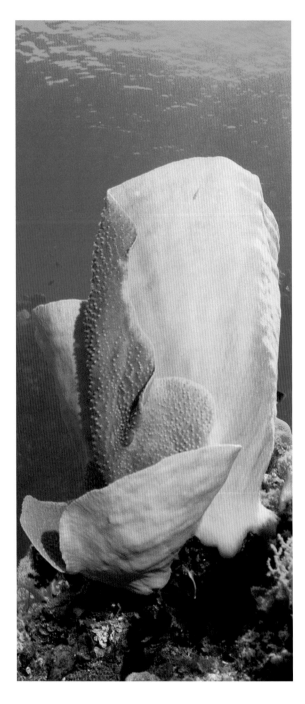

above, left to right: Vase coral; the brilliantly striped Emperor Angelfish; Feather Sea Stars feeding in the currents.
opposite: Whitehaven Beach, Hill Inlet and Tongue Point on untouched Whitsunday Island. Some of the world's best sailing can be found in the Whitsunday Passage.

Townsville and the Great Green Way

▶ ▶

Townsville was first known as Castleton but, when it was officially declared a port in 1865, it was renamed after its founder, Robert Towns. A breakwater was built in 1872 and later the harbour was dredged and a rail link built from Townsville heading west. The railway line reached Charters Towers in 1882 and ultimately to Mount Isa in the 1920s. Townsville has been the chief port for the mines of Mary Kathleen, Charters Towers and Mount Isa, as well as for pastoral produce from all the wide lands to the west and around the Gulf of Carpentaria. The city, sitting at the base of Castle Hill, has a warm, balmy climate, bright tropical gardens and views out across Cleveland Bay to the Coral Sea.

From Townsville pioneers went to all points of the compass in search of gold, timber and land. While growing into the country's largest northern city and the logical centre for much of the development of the far north, Townsville has retained the natural beauty of its surroundings and its relaxed, tropical air. The city also has a sense of autonomous identity through its distance from the capital. In this, the most decentralised State of Australia, when Townsville's locals talk guardedly of "southerners" they are just as likely to mean the people of Brisbane as those from New South Wales or Victoria.

Eight kilometres from Townsville across Cleveland Bay is Magnetic Island, brimming with sandy beaches, sheltered bays and walking tracks. The island was so named because the explorer James Cook thought its "magnetic" rocks had played havoc with his compass.

The Great Green Way starts north of Townsville, passing through canefields, orchards and forest as it runs up to Cairns through the towns of Ingham, Cardwell and Tully. Tully has one of the highest rainfalls in Australia, which makes whitewater rafting on the Tully Gorge truly exhilarating. Also to Townsville's north is Paluma Range National Park with its mix of rainforest, dry vine forest and dry open forest. The Mount Spec section of the park is rare high-altitude forest. Off the coast from Cardwell the most dramatic views are of the 1,000-metre high peaks of Hinchinbrook Island, with mangroves and forest to landward and sandy beaches to seaward. North of Cardwell is Mission Beach; four kilometres off the coast from there lies Dunk Island, a beautiful island of rainforest.

left: Magpie Geese, egrets, Brolgas and other wetland birds gather
at dusk around Townsville's Town Common Environmental Park.

Townsville

Townsville, sprawled below Castle Hill, is Queensland's third-largest city and provides a hub for smaller towns scattered throughout the north. Once just a sleepy town, during World War II the town became a major base for allied forces and its population boomed. Townsville was bombed three times during the war and the Post Office's stone clock tower was removed to prevent the building becoming a target. Today, a large armed forces population and the many students of James Cook University keep the city buzzing with life. The Strand, a palm-lined promenade along the city's shoreline, is a popular place for locals and tourists to enjoy leisurely strolls or bike rides. It boasts 2.5 km of landscaped gardens decorated with sculptures and rock pools, as well as cafés and restaurants from which relaxed diners can enjoy a cool drink while they watch the sun set over Cleveland Bay.

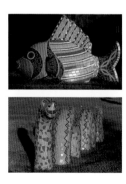

top: Overlooking the Strand. *above, left and right:* The Strand at sunrise.
this page, far right: Two of the many sculptures along the beachfront.

top: Against the backdrop of Castle Hill, private yachts and motor craft lie at their moorings in Townsville Marina.
above, left to right: Townsville Technical College is one of the city's many Heritage-listed buildings;
Townsville seen from Castle Hill Lookout; the former Townsville Post Office is now a boutique brewery.

above: Little Crystal Creek flows through Paluma Range National Park, part of the Wet Tropics World Heritage Area.

above: Arthur Bay, one of Magnetic Island's secluded bays.

Tully

Tully, halfway between Ingham and Innisfail, is arguably Australia's wettest town with an average annual rainfall of 4,200 millimetres. For this dubious honour Tully receives the nation's "Golden Gumboot" award.

The town is surrounded by lush green mountains, from which the drenching downpours flow into the Tully River, which is perfect for whitewater rafting and attracts enthusiasts from around the world. There is spectacular rainforest at Murray Falls and Alligators Nest, which is also a good picnic spot. The seemingly incessant rain and the fertile soil nourishes the region's thriving sugar cane, tea and banana crops.

left: Whitewater rafting on the Tully River is guaranteed to make the heart pump and the blood flow faster.
above: Tully's 7.9-metre-high Golden Gumboot commemorates the record-breaking rainfall recorded in 1950.

Hinchinbrook Island National Park

Just off the coast of Cardwell lies Hinchinbrook Island, where mountains cloaked in mist and emerald rainforest rise up from the jewel-bright sea.

With almost 40,000 hectares of wilderness, this is Australia's largest island national park. On its shores, beaches are secluded by rocky headlands and merge into mangroves, paperbark and palm wetlands — even, in places, to open forest and woodland. This wide habitat mix means that Hinchinbrook Island National Park is also home to many and varied species of fauna and flora. Mangroves play an integral part: they are the breeding ground for many marine species. Surrounding reefs and seagrass beds are frequented by Dugongs and turtles.

above, clockwise from top: **Off the coast of Lucinda, near the southern end of Hinchinbrook Island; mangroves are integral to Hinchinbrook Island's marine ecosystem; Goold Island, viewed from Cape Richards on Hinchinbrook Island.**
opposite: **The mountains of Hinchinbrook seen from the air.**

Mission Beach

The Mission Beach area is a 14-kilometre stretch of coastline with sandy beaches that draw ever-increasing numbers of tourists. Named after an Aboriginal mission was established there by the government in 1914, Mission Beach is a good base for trips out to the reef, visits to Dunk Island or to enjoy Tully's whitewater rafting.

The area is bordered by rainforest, part of the Northern Tropics World Heritage Area, and is resplendent with lush greenery, which in places grows right down to the beach. The scenic route to Mission Beach, along Cassowary Drive, leads through dense forests containing beautiful Fan Palms, which are necessary habitat for the endangered Southern Cassowary. The Mission Beach area contains almost half of Australia's total number of these palms. Walking tracks through Licuala State Forest, nine kilometres from Mission Beach towards Tully, provide the chance of glimpsing a cassowary, one of the region's wildlife icons.

above: The Southern Cassowary, a magnificent flightless bird, can be seen at Licuala State Forest.
right: Looking up through a stand of Fan Palms, Licuala State Forest.

Dunk Island

The Aboriginal inhabitants used to call Dunk Island *Coonanglebah*, the "Island of Peace and Plenty". The island lives up to its original name. It is almost two thirds national park, but also contains a large resort. Daytrippers will find plenty to do, whether bushwalking in the steep rainforests or swimming and relaxing on the island's lovely beaches. Dunk is renowned for its abundant birdlife and its many butterflies; the striking Ulysses Butterfly is used as the island's official logo.

left: Although mainly national park, Dunk Island also boasts a luxury resort.
above, top to bottom: Taking it easy at Dunk Island Resort; kayaking from Mission Beach to Dunk Island; the Ulysses Butterfly.

Cairns and Surrounds

▶ ▶

Cairns is the gateway to Tropical North Queensland. This thriving and dynamic city, once an isolated port for shipping gold, tin and timber from the Atherton Tableland and Hodgkinson River goldfield, now has its own international airport. Surrounded by forested hills and tropical vegetation, Cairns is known worldwide as a top tourist destination. Its architecture reflects both its history and its modernity, with the oldest section of town located at Trinity Wharf and a modern and airy shopping plaza at Pier Marketplace. On the foreshore, overlooking Trinity Inlet, the beach at Cairns Lagoon was created to provide a year-round water playground.

As well as being an interesting destination in itself, Cairns city is close to World-Heritage-listed terrestrial and marine areas, and is a good base from which to explore these wonders and many other fascinating places. The Great Barrier Reef and its exquisite coral cays are easily accessed from here. Innisfail, 83 kilometres south of Cairns, is a charming tropical town that has been relatively untouched by tourism and is a good stepping-off point for the surrounding national parks.

Port Douglas, north of Cairns, began in the 1870s as a port for the northern goldfields, but declined when the railway went through in the 1920s. However, since the 1980s, it has enjoyed a renaissance as a holiday resort. The one-hour trip from Cairns to Port Douglas is one of the most scenic coastal drives in Australia, providing gorgeous views of the Coral Sea. With luxury retreats for the wealthy as well as budget accommodation, Port Douglas is firmly on the international tourist map, not least because of its proximity to other appealing destinations: the Reef, the Daintree Rainforest, Cape Tribulation and Kuranda.

The humidity of the tropical plains lifts in the crisp atmosphere of the 900-metre-high Atherton Tableland, which has some of Australia's loveliest waterfalls and crystalline crater lakes. Here too are cool high-altitude rainforests, lush farms and captivating villages. Abundant rainfall, rich volcanic soil and the climate make the tableland a veritable food bowl, known for products ranging from coffee and macadamia nuts to sugar and milk.

left: The saltwater Cairns Lagoon on the Esplanade is protected from marine stingers and is safe for swimming throughout the year.

above, top to bottom: Along Cairns Esplanade graceful palms sway in the breeze;
a fine example of one of the city's historic buildings; modern shopping complexes abound.
right: Cairns city and harbour, situated between the rainforest and the reef.

above left: Green Island, a 15-hectare coral cay off Cairns, is known for its underwater observatory and for the abundance of sea creatures that fill its crystal-clear waters.
above, top to bottom: Feather Stars feed on plankton; a snorkeller lost in the magic of the reef.

The Great Barrier Reef stretches more than 2,000 kilometres north of Fraser Island to the Gulf of Papua.
opposite: A scuba diver with camera approaches a giant Potato Cod at the famous "Cod Hole".
above, left to right: An Orange-fin Anemonefish; the tentacles of a sea anemone shelter a Pink Anemonefish.
pages 112 and 113: The Frankland Islands, just off Cairns, are a popular daytrip destination.

Innisfail

Innisfail is a prosperous sugar-cane city sprawled at the junction of the North and South Johnstone Rivers. This is a relaxed and friendly city with pleasant parks and picnic areas in Charles Street. Innisfail's location makes it a great spot for fishing and the town supports a large aquaculture industry — prawns, barramundi and crayfish are farmed here. Further east some of Queensland's less amiable inhabitants are bred at the Johnstone River Crocodile Farm. Saltwater Crocodiles, also known as Estuarine Crocodiles, are hugely popular exhibits with tourists and locals alike.

Innisfail is also an agricultural centre for the traditional crops of the region — bananas, pawpaw and tropical fruit — and commercially grown tea was added to the list in the 1950s.

far left: Innisfail seen from the air.
left, top to bottom: Innisfail Court House; a mural in the town; Josephine Falls, Wooroonooran National Park, north-west of Innisfail.

Port Douglas

Set off by the white sands of Four Mile Beach, the town of Port Douglas is a glamorous resort close to the region's must-see tourist destinations. Despite multimillion-dollar resorts and plenty of glitz, good shopping and fine restaurants, Port Douglas has all the charm of a relaxed seaside town.

above, top to bottom: The Low Isles, off Port Douglas, are a popular mooring; Longfin Bannerfish are among the most beautiful of the Reef's many spectacular fish. *above right:* Port Douglas offers safe all-weather anchorage.

pages 118 and 119: The sand on Four Mile Beach, Port Douglas, is firm enough to land a plane, as accomplished by Australian pioneer aviator Sir Charles Kingsford Smith.

Cape Tribulation and Daintree National Park

North of Port Douglas, set in the lush tropical rainforest of Daintree National Park, is Cape Tribulation. It was named by the British explorer James Cook to mark where his troubles began on his journey along Queensland's east coast — just north of it he ran aground on what is now Endeavour Reef. The Kuku Yalanji people, whose association with the cape probably dates back to the earliest human occupation of Australia, call it *Kulki*. As part of the Wet Tropics World Heritage Area, all of Cape Tribulation's offshore waters and beautiful reefs are protected.

Daintree National Park contains some of the world's oldest and most structurally diverse forest, and the richness of the park's animal and plant life matches this environment. Both Saltwater and Freshwater Crocodiles may be spotted basking in the sun. The park also nurtures rare and unusual species, such as the Giant White-tailed Rat, the Southern Cassowary, Bennett's Tree-kangaroo and several species of primitive flowering plants.

above: The Native Rhododendron is a unique plant of the region.
above right, top to bottom: Thornton Peak, Daintree National Park; a basking Saltwater Crocodile; exposed mangrove roots at Cape Tribulation.
opposite: Cape Tribulation is clothed in tropical green rainforest that sweeps down to the sea.

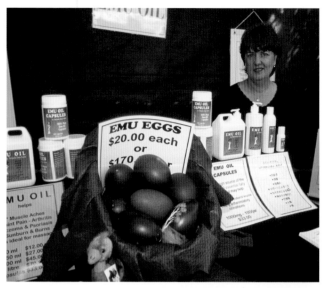

Kuranda

Kuranda is in the hills above Cairns. It is the terminus of the breathtaking 34-kilometre Scenic Railway. The railway winds its way past waterfalls and through rainforest, through 15 tunnels and over 40 bridges, travelling up the steep and dramatic scarp of the Atherton Tableland. On market days Kuranda is a hive of activity with stallholders offering goods that range from homemade jam to Emu eggs and every form of craft. Visitors to Kuranda can take the Scenic Railway one way and, on the other, enjoy the longest cable-car journey in the world, a thrilling 7.5-kilometre trip dangling above the coastal plain and forest canopy.

above, clockwise from top left: The Kuranda Skyway; the picturesque Atherton Tableland village of Kuranda has excellent markets;
Kuranda Railway Station; the Scenic Railway has carried passengers on its spectacular trip up and down the tableland since 1891.

above: The Cairns Birdwing Butterfly frequents the many walking tracks around Kuranda and can also be seen there at the Australian Butterfly Sanctuary.

Unique Plants and Wildlife of the Wet Tropics

The climate of Tropical North Queensland is characterised by summers of high humidity and heavy rains followed by mild, dryer winters — this, combined with the rich soil, has created many different habitat niches. The amazing range of wildlife supported by these habitats can really only be understood with a quick dose of statistics from the Commonwealth Department of Environment and Heritage: the Wet Tropics World Heritage Area is home to 58 per cent of Australia's bat species, 30 per cent of Australia's marsupial species, 26 per cent of its frog species, 17 per cent of its reptile species, 58 per cent of its butterflies and 48 per cent of its birds. No less than 58 species of vertebrates are unique to the area. At least 390 species of plants are classified as rare or restricted, 74 of these as threatened.

above, clockwise from left: The Striped Possum, active at night, is a rainforest resident and the only tree-dwelling mammal to have bold stripes; the Red-eyed Tree-Frog is usually only seen after heavy rain; a male Australian King-Parrot; the arboreal Green Python can grow to 1.7 metres but is harmless to humans. *opposite:* In the World Heritage Area of Wooroonooran National Park, fringing the eastern side of the Atherton Tableland, the more ancient plants have remained unchanged for millions of years.

above, top to bottom: The Grand Hotel in Atherton's main street; a grand sweep of the rural tableland; the Malanda Hotel, Malanda.

The Atherton Tableland

Perched high between the Bellenden Ker and Great Dividing Ranges is the Atherton Tableland, where the elevation ranges between 600 and 1,100 metres. Some of Australia's richest agricultural land and most splendid rainforest coexists here, and biologists coined the phrase "the greatest celebration of life on earth" to describe the wealth of plant and animal life in the Wet Tropics. Alongside World-Heritage-listed rainforests, mountains, waterfalls, rocky rivers and national parks are charming villages and towns that serve the rural population, process and ship produce and cater for visitors.

The Atherton Tableland is the food bowl of the north. On the rich and fertile plains vegetables, grains, tea and fruit are grown and dairy cows graze. Forestry, now being managed as a plantation industry, has long been part of the region's economy. Black Bean and walnut from the tableland were used in the restoration of the British House of Commons after World War II.

Atherton, the region's principal town and its business centre, is the hub for business, shopping, dining and entertainment. Ravenshoe, to the south, is Queensland's highest altitude town. It was built on the back of the timber industry but, with the Heritage-listing of forests in 1987, it has been reinvented as a creative and cultural retreat for artists and writers. Craft shops and art galleries display the area's considerable output while the annual October Festival of the Forests celebrates its wood crafts.

clockwise from left: The spectacular Curtain Fig Tree near Yungaburra; the classic drop of Millaa Millaa Falls, one of the many waterfalls on the Atherton Tableland; looking out over tranquil Lake Eacham.

Cape York and The Gulf

▶ ▶

For most travellers Cooktown marks the beginning of the unforgettable trip north up "The Cape", where the journey is an integral part of the adventure. This vast region experiences extremes of climate and terrain where there are only two seasons: the Wet and the Dry. It is one of the world's largest wilderness areas, dotted with just a few communities. It encompasses rugged mountains, grassland, largely untouched rainforest, monsoon forest, and wet and dry eucalypt woodland, along with estuaries and wild coastline. The single road to Cape York Peninsula, the most northerly landfall on the Australian mainland, is open only during the Dry and traverses large tracts of Aboriginal land. In 1644 the Dutch navigator Abel Tasman named this triangular promontory Carpentaria Land. Today the best access is by four-wheel-drive vehicle or by boat from the Torres Strait. The significant Aboriginal sites in the region include important rock art. The Quinkan Galleries, with their magnificent clay and ochre paintings, are believed to have been frequented by local Aborigines for more than 13,000 years.

In 1770 British explorer James Cook and his crew came ashore to repair the *Endeavour* on the banks of what is now known as the Endeavour River. More than one hundred years later nearby Cooktown was founded when gold was discovered on the Palmer River. The town is now mainly a tourist centre for the wilderness beyond.

To the south-west of Cape York the Gulf savannah is impassable in the Wet, hot and parched by the middle of the Dry. The Gulf is cattle country — stockhorses are still crucial for mustering and inspecting the more rugged parts of the huge stations.

Burketown, Normanton and Karumba are the main towns in this vast flatness, with beef roads linking the first two. The Gulf of Carpentaria prawning industry is centred in Karumba, known for great fishing and even greater Saltwater Crocodiles. The Gulf's shores and plains are home to pelicans, wallabies and wallaroos, and the coast is dream country for fishers and birdwatchers. The Gulflander, a venerable motor rail, makes the 94-kilometre, four-hour trip from Normanton to Croydon, a historic goldmining town, each Wednesday. Travellers can overnight in Croydon and return the following day. Further east are the world's longest lava tubes at Undara Volcanic National Park.

left: Mudflats and mangrove forests dominate the coastline of the Gulf of Carpentaria.

Cooktown

James Cook and his crew camped on the banks of the Endeavour River for 48 days to carry out the repairs to his ship. Each June the Endeavour Festival commemorates his landing, as well as giving the citizens good cause to celebrate.

In the late 1870s during the gold rushes, Cooktown was at its peak. Its main street stretched for two kilometres and the town had a population of some 18,000, which included 6,000 Chinese people. St Mary's Convent, built 1887–89, now houses the James Cook Historical Museum, which documents the area's natural history, Aboriginal and pioneering history, and the glories of the gold rush days.

left, top to bottom: A view of the Endeavour River, Cooktown and the hinterland from Grassy Hill; the town's monument to its namesake, the explorer James Cook; the Milibi Wall, a traditional collage constructed by local Aboriginal artists.
above: Cooktown Lighthouse glows in the afternoon light.
opposite: Charlotte Street is Cooktown's main street.

  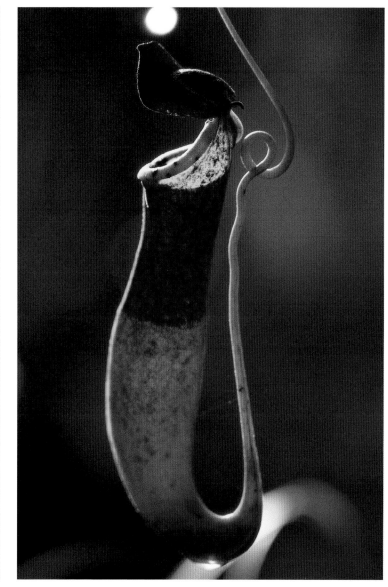

Cape York

Cape York Peninsula is varied in terrain: there are extensive wetlands on the west coast and to the east lies the Great Dividing Range. The peninsula holds some of the most inhospitable, rugged country in Australia. It is also some of the most untouched and beautiful, set with patches of rainforest, rivers and streams. The sheer assortment of landscapes, colours, birds and animals is captivating. Before European settlement Aboriginal and Torres Strait Island people shared the Cape, and now it and the Torres Strait Islands hold many tracts of native-title-designated land. Weipa, on the Cape's western coast, is a remote mining community set up to exploit the world's largest deposits of bauxite ore, which, when processed, produces aluminium.

opposite: Cape Flattery coastline. *above, left to right:* The beautiful Sacred Lotus, emblematic of the freshwater wetlands of northern Australia; a female Eclectus Parrot — small flocks congregate in noisy groups in tall rainforest trees; the insect-eating Pitcher Plant grows in the wet highland heath country of Iron Range National Park, near the town of Lockhart River.

above: Normanton's Railway Station is Heritage-listed.

The Gulf Country

The wide, spreading land of the Gulf savannah is hot, tough country speckled with scrubby bush and saltpans and dotted with isolated small towns, Aboriginal communities and cattle stations. Tidal rivers flow into the massive curve of the Gulf, crocodile country fringed with mud and mangroves. In the Wet most of the roads are cut. If supplies run out expensive air freight is the only reliable way to get goods in.

above, clockwise from top: The "Purple Pub", a famed local watering hole in Normanton; the Gulflander travels through some of Queensland's most remote country; road trains carry cattle and goods to and from far-flung towns; a solitary campsite is not hard to find in this wide, brown land; Karumba is the Gulf of Carpentaria's major fishing port.

Undara Volcanic National Park

Undara Volcanic National Park is unique: as well as a variety of wildlife, the park contains the longest lava tube cave system in existence. Almost 190,000 years ago a violent volcanic eruption covered the surrounding landscape, filling a valley to the north-west with a 160-kilometre lava flow. While the surface lava cooled to a crust, the lava within continued to flow away, like water within a pipe, and formed tunnels within rock. Over the years weaker sections of the roof have collapsed. Bats and owls nest in the caves of this unusual geographic feature, and between 35 and 40 cave-dwelling species are known to be there.

left: A lava tube in Undara Volcanic National Park.
above, clockwise from top left: Ghost Bats roosting in caves; a curious female Antilopine Wallaroo; an Agile Wallaby; the nocturnal Sugar Glider.

The Outback

▶ ▶

It is generally agreed that the Outback covers most of Australia beyond the ranges, from the monsoon-affected north to the parched centre and south. But it is more a feeling than an actual place. If asked, "Where does the Outback begin?" everyone will give a different answer. And it will probably be just a bit further over the horizon. Nonetheless it can hardly be argued that the great swathe of Queensland from The Gulf down to the Channel Country is part of the Outback. With climatic extremes — floods and drought, heat and cold, fire and frost — the people who live here must be determined and resilient. This is the land of drovers, swaggies, graziers, stockhands and duffers, all supreme bush men and women, with the skill and the will to raise cattle in this difficult country. Struggle and defeat, heartbreak and love for the harsh, beautiful landscape are captured by Australia's famed bush poets, Henry Lawson and Banjo Paterson. Paterson is said to have penned *Waltzing Matilda* on Dagworth Station, near Winton. The Australian Stockman's Hall of Fame and Outback Heritage Centre at Longreach lauds the men and women of the bush.

The red soil of Mount Isa, a thriving mining town, covers the underlying mineral riches, while to the east, in Hughenden, more riches are unearthed: the bones of dinosaurs. To the east is Charters Towers, to the south-east are Winton and Barcaldine, while in the west is Boulia, on the edge of the Simpson Desert, where the ghostly Min Min light hovers in the night. The first documented sighting was by a horseman travelling between Boulia and Winton in 1912. Mesmerising or terrifying, explanations of it range from fire flies to Aboriginal spirits or atmospheric forces, and include gas escaping from artesian bores and an inverted mirage of light sources hundreds of kilometres away.

The Channel Country is often desert and many have failed in the bone-dry years, leaving with nothing but shattered dreams; yet heavy rains can transform the landscape. The myriad channels of the Diamantina River and Cooper Creek criss-cross the plains, then turn into inland lakes: the flow creeps towards Lake Eyre, but often soaks into the parched land before it gets there. Rich grasses crowd the sparse spinifex, brightly coloured wildflowers spring forth and birds and animals rush to breed while the good weather lasts.

left: Between red sandstone walls, the cool, clear water of Lawn Hill Gorge, Boodjamulla (Lawn Hill) National Park, has created an oasis in the parched land.

Charters Towers and Ravenswood

Charters Towers is a former gold rush town. Because of its wealth, it operated the only Stock Exchange in Australia that was not based in a capital city. Fortune hunters from far and wide came to try their luck in the burgeoning town, which in those days was known as "The World" because anything one needed could be found there. Today, many fine buildings from its rich past grace its streets and it survives as an important centre for the beef industry.

In 1900, gold was struck at Ravenswood, east of Charters Towers. The town flourished, but was largely abandoned once the treasure ran low. It is has since returned to life, and its historic buildings, which include an old post office, court house and police station, are evidence of the riches come and gone. The elegant pubs usually shelter a few friendly, relaxed locals who will happily spin many a good yarn about Ravenswood's glory days.

opposite and this page, top: Many buildings in Charters Towers survive from the gold rush.
this page, above: Wrought iron decorates the balcony of the Railway Hotel, Ravenswood.

Getting Around the Outback

Isolation is the inescapable reality of the Outback. Even today land travel is arduous and travellers are at the mercy of difficult terrain and unpredictable weather. The challenges of transport between Outback communities and the rest of Australia were first met by the remarkable "ships of the desert", camels. First brought to Australia in 1840, the camels were vital until rail and road systems improved. But the most dramatic change to travel around the Outback came with aviation. Qantas, Australia's national airline, was established in Winton in 1920, the result of remarkable pioneering spirit and determination that changed life in the Outback forever.

above: The hangar housing the Qantas Founders Outback Museum in Longreach was the first operational base for Australia's aviation industry.

above: Camels helped open up the often drought-stricken Outback. Wild herds remain; while domesticated stock, like this camel at Winton, are used for recreational travel.

Succour in the Desert

The Outback's history and its very essence are reflected in the character of its pubs. For those who live in tiny towns at the back of beyond, or on large cattle stations, the nearest pub is the noisy, spirited heart of the community. In droving days, many a hotel resounded with music, laughter, and even cheers following a good yarn, with thirsty jackaroos relaying tales first heard around the campfire. Today, in a region where summer temperatures swelter around 40° Celsius, not much has changed. From Cunnamulla to Charleville, Blackall to Barcaldine, every pub in Outback Queensland has a unique tale to tell.

In 1892, the single-story wooden Wellshot Hotel at Ilfracombe arrived from Barcaldine on the back of a bullock cart! In September, Birdville's population increases from 120 to several thousand for the Birdsville Cup Race Meeting, and the amber liquid flows readily at the famous hotel.

Some Hotels are authentically named, such as the Blue Heeler and the Outback Hotel. Most sprawl, cool and inviting, the outside emblazoned with signs advertising Queensland's State-produced Castlemaine Fourex and the bars inside festooned with memorabilia.

above and bottom left: The famous Birdsville Hotel is a welcome sight in the remote Outback.
bottom, centre to right: Memorabilia inside Kynuna's Blue Heeler Hotel; the real thing waits patiently outside.

above, clockwise from top left: The Outback Hotel, Thargomindah; Barcaldine's Globe Hotel; Nindigully Hotel (1863), near St George; Wellshot Hotel, Ilfracombe; Quamby Hotel, Quamby; the Central, Cloncurry; Winton's Tattersalls Hotel; the Central and Welcome Home Hotels, Longreach.

this page and opposite: The buildings and homes of the Outback reflect the region's tough, formidable character. Sprawling and desolate, many are reminiscent of the scattered, sun-bleached bones of stock after a long drought. That they remain inhabited is testimony to the tenacity and resourcefulness of the Outback people, who will never waste anything that still has good use in it.

above, left to right: The Dig Tree, a coolibah on the western side of Cooper Creek near the Queensland–South Australia border, was where supplies were buried for Burke and Wills on their tragic expedition. It stood for 140 years, a symbol of a harsh country and the courage of explorers who blazed its trails, until 2002 when vandals set it alight; the Tree of Knowledge at Barcaldine marks the site where the Australian Labor Party was founded in 1891.

above, left and right: Combo Waterhole near Winton. It is said that near here, "camped by a billabong" on Dagworth Station at Winton, A.B. "Banjo" Paterson wrote the famous Australian ballad *Waltzing Matilda*. The ballad was first performed in public at Winton's North Gregory Hotel in 1895.

Wildlife and Wild Places

The area around the Simpson Desert, in the red and arid south-west of Queensland, is home to a number of animals specifically adapted for the variations in temperature and habitat. Whether gibber desert, hummock grassland, red sandy dune or flooded wet-season swampland, wildlife unique to the habitat can be found.

Some of the continent's rare carnivorous marsupials, such as the Mulgara and the Fat-tailed Dunnart, live in burrows in the desert by day and emerge at dusk to hunt in the cool of night. Blood vessels close to the surface of the Bilby's large ears enable the animal to reduce its body heat without losing moisture so that it also can survive in the harsh landscape. Here, too, lives Australia's largest mammalian predator, the Dingo, as well as the world's largest marsupial, the Red Kangaroo.

top: The endangered Bilby (known as the Greater Bilby until the Lesser Bilby became extinct) is a cat-sized burrowing marsupial.
above, left to right: The mouse-like Mulgara is an active predator with a crest of black hairs on its tail; the Fat-tailed Dunnart can be recognised by its big ears and fat tail. It uses the fat as a food reserve.

above, clockwise from top left: The Outback is riddled with winding river channels that flood during heavy wet seasons, rendering large tracts of land impassable; dune systems and spinifex, Simpson Desert National Park, 100 kilometres west of Birdsville; gibber desert and hummock grassland stretch for thousands of kilometres; Moonda Lake, part of a lake system roughly between Birdsville and Betoota in the Outback.

The Ancient Past

Underneath the Outback's hard exterior lies the evidence, hidden for aeons, of the ancestry of modern Australian wildlife. Richmond and Hughenden are situated on what was once the Cretaceous Inland Sea. Kronosaurus Korner at Richmond displays a selection of the many marine fossils found around the area, including a 100-million-year-old *Pliosaur*. Hughenden was home to terrestrial as well as marine dinosaurs; their prehistoric remains can be viewed at the Flinders Discovery Centre and Dinosaur Display Centre. On Riversleigh Station, north of Mount Isa, the fossilised remains of carnivorous kangaroos, marsupial lions and huge carnivorous birds from more than thirty million years ago are preserved at the World-Heritage-listed Riversleigh Fossils Site, part of Boodjamulla (Lawn Hill) National Park.

above: The *Muttaburrasaurus* stands in front of Hughenden's Grand Hotel.
opposite: Kronosaurus Korner in Richmond is a marine fossil museum.

The History of the Outback

Queensland's Outback is best known for being the home of the State's pioneering stockmen, and the Australian Stockman's Hall of Fame at Longreach pays homage to the stalwarts of the Outback: the explorers, Aborigines, stockmen, bushrangers, poets, drovers, swaggies, squatters and graziers who created the ethos of the Outback, bare-handedly building fences, stockyards, sheds and houses, digging dams, sinking bores, raising windmills, all seeming simply to emerge quite naturally from the red dirt. Modernity, with helicopter mustering and transport by road train, may have reduced the need for droving but, when drought bites, mobs still take to the "long paddock", the stock routes, in search of feed. On many cattle stations the stockman's spirit survives — the cattle are still mustered on horseback across paddocks large and small. The statue in front of the Hall of Fame is of a trudging stockman carrying his saddle and bridle, an image of Queensland's ongoing Outback traditions.

left: Mustering in the Outback.
above: The Australian Stockman's Hall of Fame at Longreach.
pages 156 and 157: Spectacular Porcupine Creek National Park.

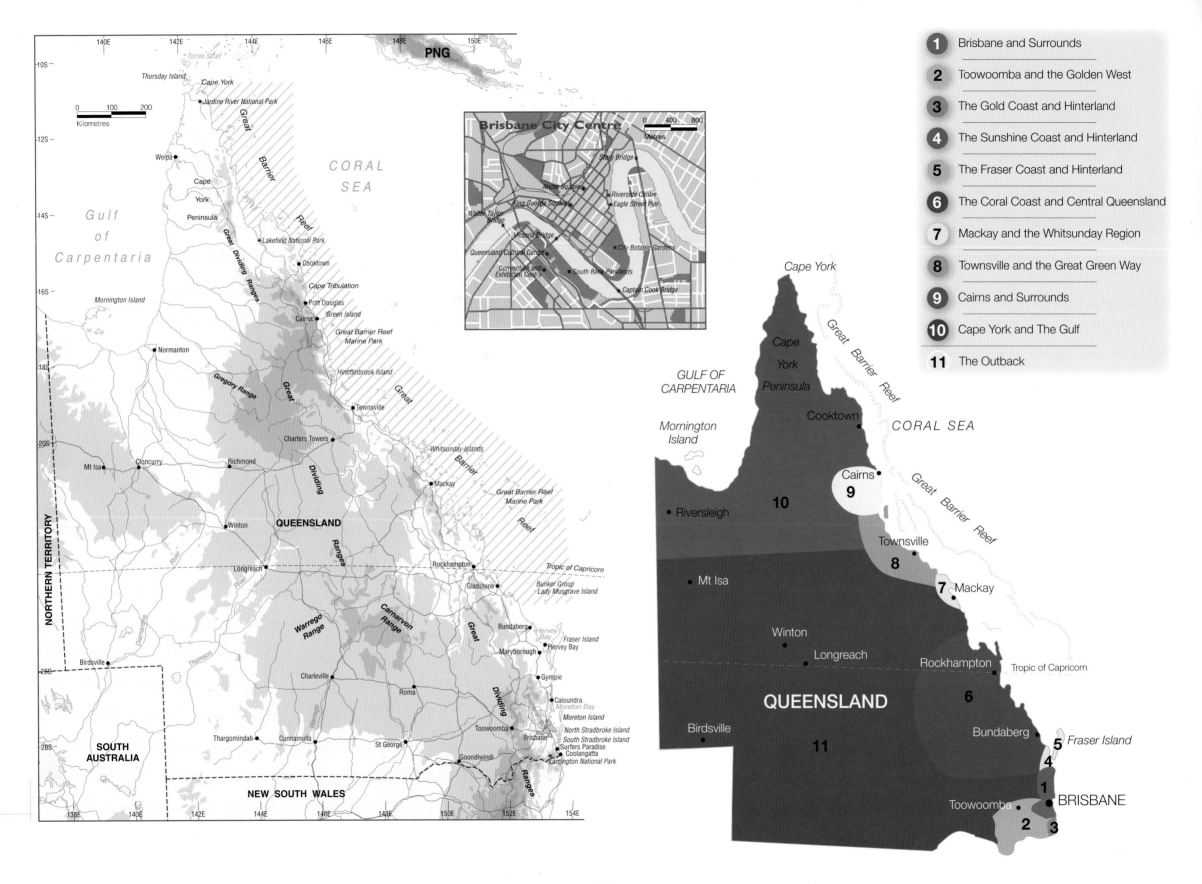

1 Brisbane and Surrounds

2 Toowoomba and the Golden West

3 The Gold Coast and Hinterland

4 The Sunshine Coast and Hinterland

5 The Fraser Coast and Hinterland

6 The Coral Coast and Central Queensland

7 Mackay and the Whitsunday Region

8 Townsville and the Great Green Way

9 Cairns and Surrounds

10 Cape York and The Gulf

11 The Outback

Index

above: High-rise buildings line the beaches of Queensland's Gold Coast.

Published by Steve Parish Publishing Pty Ltd
PO Box 1058, Archerfield, Queensland 4108 Australia

www.steveparish.com.au

© copyright Steve Parish Publishing Pty Ltd

ISBN 978174021673 9

First published 2005. Reprinted 2010.

Photography: Steve Parish

Additional photography:
pp. 10-11, Greg Harm; p. 12 (Goodwill Bridge), Emma Harm;
p. 60 (Gympie Gold Mining and Historical Museum), Raoul Slater;
p. 137 (Ghost Bat) and p. 150, Ian Morris

Text: Wynne Webber

Proofreading: Kerry Davies

Publisher: Donald Greig

Maps supplied by MAPGraphics, Australia

Film by Colour Chiefs Digital Imaging, Brisbane, Australia
Printed in China by Printplus Limited

Produced in Australia at the Steve Parish Publishing Studios